Sharks and Dolphins

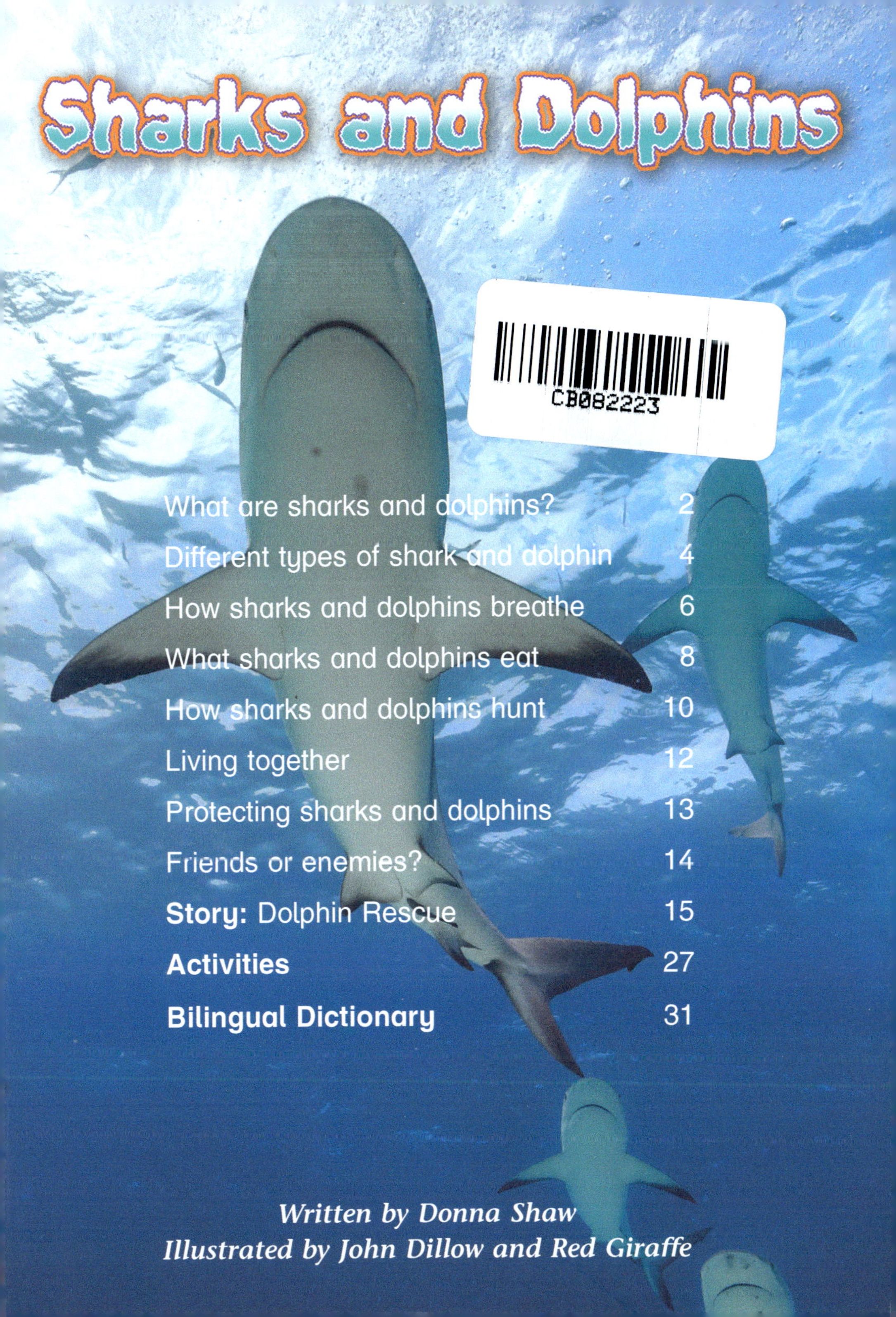

CB082223

Written by Donna Shaw
Illustrated by John Dillow and Red Giraffe

What are sharks and dolphins?

Sharks and dolphins both live in the sea, but they are very different.

Sharks are fish. They are cold-blooded. Their skin is sharp, like teeth. Sharks have got a very strong tail. They move their tail from side to side when they swim. Many sharks have got two fins on their back.

The tail moves from side to side.

Dolphins are mammals. They are warm-blooded and have got soft skin. Dolphins have got a strong tail, too. Dolphins move their tail up and down when they swim. Almost all dolphins have got a fin on their back.

The tail moves up and down.

Different types of shark and dolphin

There are many different types of shark and dolphin. There are about 340 types of shark. You can find sharks in the sea and some sharks can swim in rivers, too. The biggest shark is the Whale Shark. It is more than twelve metres long.

A Whale Shark

The smallest shark is the Pygmy Lantern Shark. It is only twenty-two centimetres long.

A Pygmy Lantern Shark

There are about 57 types of dolphin. The biggest dolphin is the Orca. It is sometimes called a Killer Whale. It lives in the sea and is nine metres long.

An Orca Dolphin

The smallest dolphin is the Tucuxi Dolphin. It lives in the Amazon River and is about one metre long.

A Tucuxi Dolphin

How sharks and dolphins breathe

Sharks and dolphins need oxygen. Sharks breathe water. The water has got oxygen in it. Sharks don't breathe through their nose. They breathe through gills. All sharks have got five or more pairs of gills on each side of their head.

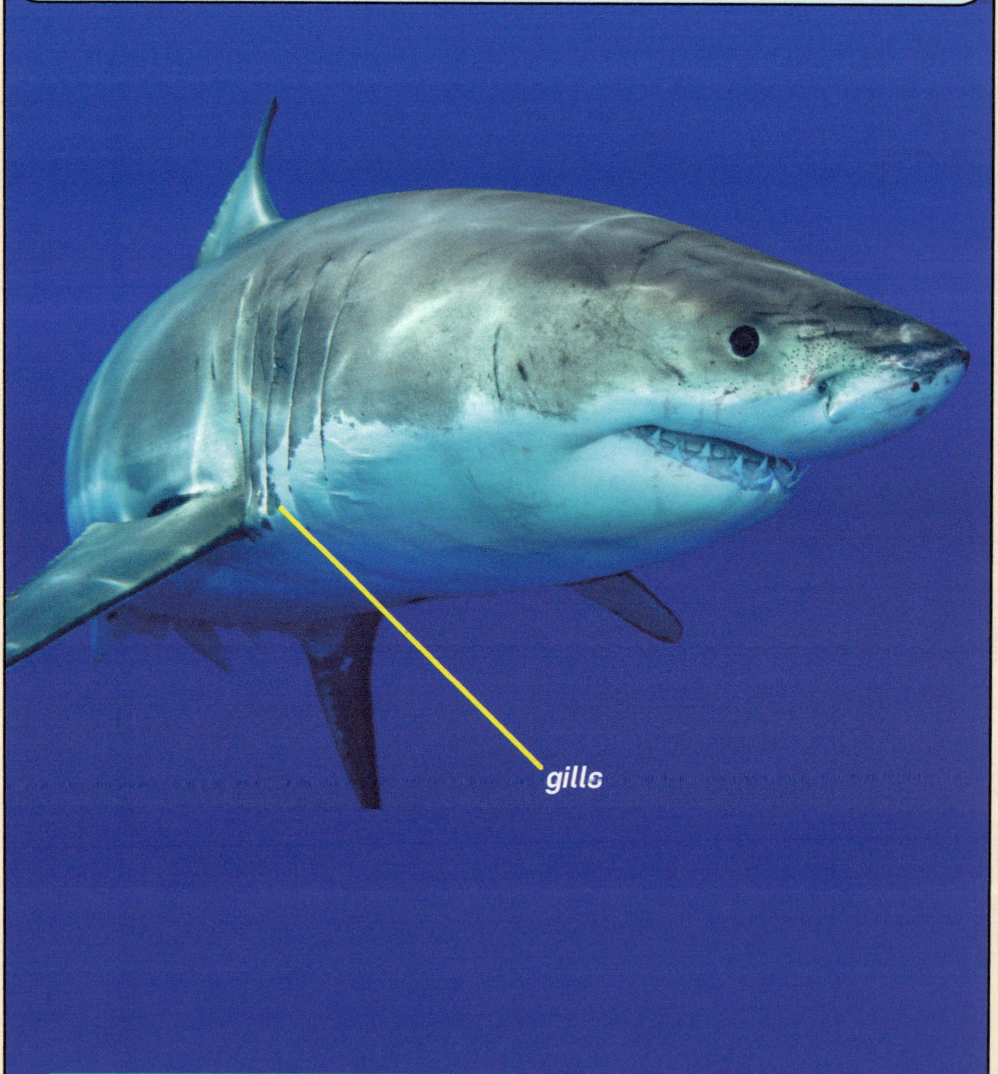

Sharks breathe through their gills.

Dolphins breathe air. They breathe through a hole on the top of their head. It is called a blowhole. Dolphins put their head out of the sea every time they breathe. A dolphin can stay under the water for about ten minutes.

Dolphins breathe through their blowhole.

What sharks and dolphins eat

Sharks eat all kinds of sea animals. They eat fish, crabs and prawns. Big sharks eat seals, dolphins and smaller sharks, too.

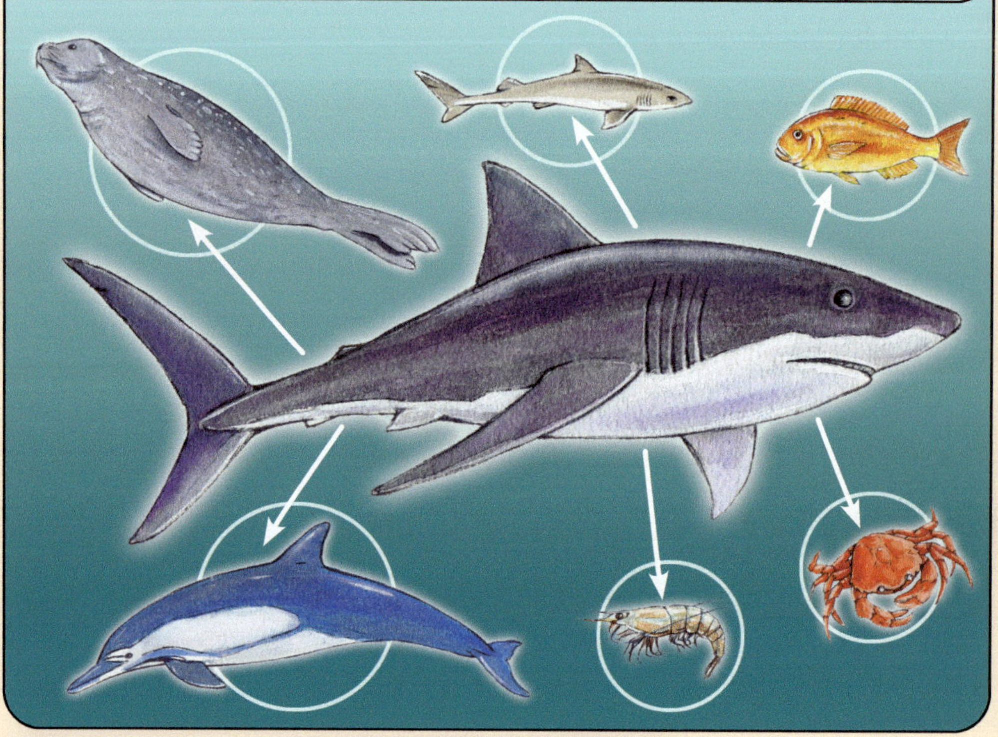

A shark can have 3000 teeth. When a shark's tooth falls out, another one grows in its place.

Dolphins eat fish and squid. They use their teeth to bite their food, but they don't chew it. They eat their food whole.

A Bottlenose Dolphin has around 80 to 90 teeth.

How sharks and dolphins hunt

Sharks and dolphins hunt for food. Sharks are excellent hunters. They can hear and see very well. They can smell a tiny bit of blood in the sea. Sharks can feel vibrations in the water, too.

Sharks are excellent hunters.

Dolphins are very good hunters, too. They can hear and see very well, but they can't smell very well. Dolphins use sound to find food. They make special noises and listen to the echo.

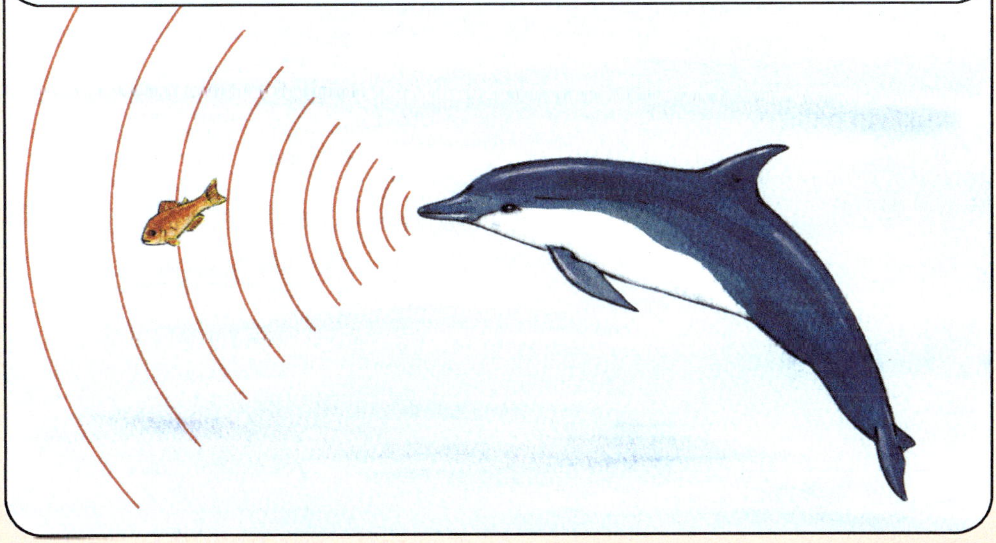

Dolphins use sound to find food.

Living together

Sharks aren't sociable animals. They are usually solitary. They don't live in groups. They live and hunt on their own.

Sharks are solitary animals.

Dolphins are usually very sociable. They live in family groups. The adult dolphins protect the young and weak dolphins in the group. They make noises to communicate with each other.

Dolphins play and hunt together.

Protecting sharks and dolphins

Dolphins and sharks live in the sea together. Sharks sometimes attack and kill dolphins. A group of dolphins can sometimes attack and kill a shark. However, the biggest danger for sharks and dolphins is humans. Humans pollute the sea with chemicals and rubbish. We need to protect sharks and dolphins.

Humans pollute the sea.

Friends or enemies?

Sharks do not normally attack people. There are about 340 species of shark, but only about 25 species are dangerous. In some marine parks sharks are protected. Biologists study how the sharks live. People go there to swim with the sharks.

Most sharks aren't dangerous.

Dolphins are intelligent and sociable. In some places around the world dolphins like swimming with people. In Monkey Mia, in Australia, you can swim with the dolphins and feed them.

Dolphins are usually friendly.

Dolphin Rescue

Written by Donna Shaw
Illustrated by John Dillow

James and Annie live in Australia. One day they were at home with their mum. It was the summer holidays. It was too hot to play football and they didn't want to do their homework. They decided to go to the beach.
It's too hot today!
I've got a good idea. Why don't we go surfing?
Remember! Only swim near the lifeguards and put some sun cream on.

James and Annie carried their surfboards to the beach. There was a green flag on the beach. Lots of people were swimming and playing in the sea. Their friends, Tim and Claire, were on the beach. They weren't very happy.

So they decided to go to another beach. They carried their surfboards over the rocks. There wasn't a green flag on the other beach, but the waves were bigger.

Tim, Claire and Annie put their swimsuits on. Then they ran into the sea with their surfboards. The three friends laughed and jumped in the waves. James didn't want to surf. He was angry with his friends.
I'm not going to surf here. It's too dangerous.
Don't be silly, James.
Come on, James! These waves are fantastic.

James climbed onto the rocks and watched his friends in the sea. The waves were very big. Tim fell off his surfboard and the girls laughed. But James wasn't very happy. He wanted to be with his friends, but he knew it was dangerous.

Suddenly, James saw a big, grey fish near the rocks. It swam very fast and it had a fin on its back. It was a shark!

James was very scared. He watched the shark swim towards his three friends. He waved his arms and shouted, but they didn't hear him. He shouted again and again.

Suddenly, some dolphins appeared next to Annie, Tim and Claire. The dolphins swam in circles around the three friends. The dolphins made lots of noise and hit the water with their tails. Annie, Tim and Claire were very surprised.

Then the friends saw the shark. The shark opened its mouth and tried to attack, but the dolphins protected the children. The dolphins swam faster and faster and made lots of noise. The children shouted for help.

James climbed down the rocks and ran to the next beach. He saw the two lifeguards on the beach and quickly ran to them.

The lifeguards got in their boat and went to find the three friends. The boat moved quickly through the water. James ran back to the other beach. He was very worried.

A few minutes later the lifeguards found Annie, Tim and Claire. They were on their surfboards, but the shark wasn't there. Six dolphins jumped and played around the children. The children were very happy when they saw the lifeguards.

The lifeguards pulled the children into the boat and took them back to the beach. The dolphins followed the boat to the beach.

The lifeguards were angry with the children. The children were very sorry and Claire started to cry.

The Australian News

Dolphin Rescue

A family of dolphins save children from a shark.

The children were surfing in the sea when a three-metre shark swam towards them. Then six dolphins appeared and swam around the children to protect them from the shark. Two lifeguards rescued the children. A biologist said, "Dolphins can help and protect smaller and weaker animals. The children were very lucky."

Activities

1 Find, circle and write the words.

1 

shark

2 

______

3 

______

4 

______

5 

______

6 

______

7 

______

8 

______

s	h	a	r	k	r	r
z	r	w	x	d	u	d
t	r	g	y	h	b	o
o	a	f	i	n	b	l
o	b	l	p	q	i	p
t	t	a	i	l	s	h
h	s	e	d	c	h	i
s	q	u	i	d	g	n

2 Read the sentences. Then write *dolphins*, *sharks*, **or** *both* **(dolphins and sharks).**

1 They move their tails up and down.

dolphins

2 They move their tails from side to side.

______

3 They eat fish.

______

4 They have gills.

______

5 They can hunt very well.

______

6 They usually hunt on their own.

______

7 They communicate with each other.

______

8 They need to be protected.

______

3 Complete the sentences with the numbers in the box.

340	9	3000	10	12	5

1 There are about ___340___ types of shark.

2 The biggest shark is the Whale Shark. It is more than ________ metres long.

3 The biggest dolphin is the Orca. It is ________ metres long.

4 All sharks have got ________ or more pairs of gills on each side of their head.

5 A dolphin can stay under the water for about ________ minutes.

6 A shark can have ________ teeth.

4 Look at the notes and write about the Great White Shark.

Great White Sharks are about six metres long.

____

____

____

____

____

____

____

5 Match the adjectives to the pictures.

happy ~~silly~~ suprised scared angry worried

1 silly

2 ______

3 ______

4 ______

5 ______

6 ______

6 Who said it? Match the sentences to the pictures.

1 Don't be silly, James.

2 Come on, James! These waves are fantastic.

3 But there isn't a lifeguard here. It's dangerous.

4 We're here to help you. Are you okay?

5 There aren't any big waves.

7 Complete the story with the words in the box.

beach ~~decided~~ waves appeared ran shouted saw wanted sat said

One day last summer, James and Annie (1) _decided_ to go to the beach. They (2) ____________ to go surfing. They met Claire and Tim on the (3) ____________. Claire and Tim were sad because there weren't any big (4) ____________. They went to the next beach, but James didn't want to surf because there wasn't a lifeguard. James (5) ____________ on some rocks. He (6) ____________ a shark and (7) ____________ to his friends, but they didn't hear him. Some dolphins (8) ____________ and swam around the children. James (9) ____________ to the next beach and told the lifeguards. The lifeguards found the children and took them back to the beach. The friends (10) ____________ sorry to the lifeguards, and to James.

8 A newspaper reporter is asking James about the rescue. Order and write the questions.

1 you / beach / Did / yesterday / go / the / to?
Did you go to the beach yesterday?

2 swim / you / Did ? ____________________

3 you / surf / Did ? ____________________

4 see / you / shark / Did / the ? ____________________

5 dolphins / Did / make / the / noise / a ? ____________________

6 shark / the / attack / Did / friends / your ? ____________________

Bilingual Dictionary

Write the words in your language.

angry	______	prawn	______
attack	______	protect	______
beach	______	quickly	______
biologist	______	rescue	______
blood	______	rock	______
blowhole	______	rubbish	______
breathe	______	scared	______
chemicals	______	seal	______
chew	______	sharp	______
cold-blooded	______	skin	______
crab	______	sociable	______
dangerous	______	soft	______
fin	______	solitary	______
gills	______	squid	______
hunt	______	sun cream	______
kill	______	surfboard	______
lifeguard	______	surprised	______
lucky	______	tiny	______
mammal	______	warm-blooded	______
oxygen	______	waved	______
pollute	______	waves	______

Macmillan Education
4 Crinan Street
London N1 9XW
A division of Springer Nature Limited
Companies and representatives throughout the world

978-1-3800-3780-0

Text © Donna Shaw 2007
Design and illustration © Springer Nature Limited 2019

The author has asserted their right to be identified as the author of this work in accordance with the Copyright, Designs and Patents Act 1988.

First published 2007
This edition published in 2019

All rights reserved; no part of this publication may be reproduced, stored in a retrieval system, transmitted in any form, or by any means, electronic, mechanical, photocopying, recording, or otherwise, without the prior written permission of the publishers.

Designed by Red Giraffe Limited
Illustrated by John Dillow and Red Giraffe Limited

The author and publishers would like to thank the following for permission to reproduce their photographs:

Cover photography reproduced with the kind permission of Alamy Stock Photo/Chris & Monique Fallows

Alamy/ Water Frame p4b, Alamy Stock Photo/Norbert Probst pp12t, 14, Alamy Stock Photo/ Stéphane ROCHON p12b; Ardea/ Johan de Meester p9; Frank Lane Picture Agency/ Fred Bavendam/ Minden Pictures p2; Getty Images/by wildestanimal p1, Getty Images/Anna Phillips p8, Getty Images/Brian Kennedy p13, Getty Images / Nancy Brown p14b, Getty Images/slowmotiongli p5t, Getty Images/iStock/crisod p4(t), Getty Images/iStockphoto/Thinkstock Images/joebelanger p6, Getty Images/Moment/ Tim Melling p7; Oxford Scientific Film/ David B Fleetham pp3, 10, OSF/ Norbert Wu p11.

Printed and bound in Brazil

2025
12